SHORTS

A Gateway Into New Markets

COLLEEN FOYE BOLLEN

TURTLE ISLAND PRESS

All rights reserved. No part of this book may be reproduced or transmitted in any form or by any means, electronic or mechanical, including photocopying, recording, or by any information storage and retrieval system, without permission from the author, except for the inclusion of brief quotations in a review.

Shorts: A Gateway Into New Markets
Copyright (c) 1996 Colleen Foye Bollen

Design and cover by Constance Bollen

ISBN: 0-9654384-0-6

Manufactured in the United States of America

First Edition

TURTLE ISLAND PRESS
P.O. Box 77598
Seattle, WA 98177
E-mail CBollen@AOL.com

*This book is dedicated to my husband, Alan,
and our sons, Zander and Spencer.
Thank you for being a part of my writing adventure.*

Contents

Preface 7
Acknowledgments 13

Chapter One—What Are Shorts?
Why bother with shorts 15
Strut your stuff 16
Doable 16
Good money 17
Learn the inner workings of publications 18
The you-never-know factor 21

Chapter Two—Market Research
Who buys shorts? 23
Write what you like to read 24
Get the scoop on publications 25
Hunting and gathering 27
Detective work 29
Slanting ideas to the right market 30

Chapter Three—Nuts and Bolts
How to write a query 33
Finding the puzzle pieces 36
Asking the right questions 37

Chapter Four—Secrets to Writing Short

Stay focused 39
First draft, second draft, third draft and more 41
Draw people in 42
Cooking it down 46

Chapter Five—Final Touches

Ways to shorten phrases 49
Manuscript preparation 50
Ouch, that hurts 50
No response 52
Learning from bad experiences 53

Chapter Six—Now That You Are Published

Market yourself 55
Writing for CD ROMs 56
Greeting cards 57
Using the leftovers 57

Chapter Seven—Precious Nuggets

Ask editors for input 59
Support groups 60
Writer's block 61
Dream on 62
Writing exercises 64
When all is said and done 65

Glossary 67
Appendix A.1

Preface

This book is for people looking for a way to break into new markets. It is also a book for people who want to improve their writing skills by learning to write short. Whichever group you belong to, writing short articles will teach you valuable writing skills, such as creating strong lead paragraphs, developing a solid focus, condensing volumes of material, cutting unnecessary words, and sticking to your word limit.

I got started writing shorts by happenstance. After accumulating a jackpot-size collection of rejection slips for feature-length ideas, I tried sending editors ideas for short articles. Suddenly, I had plenty of work. Between 1994 and 1996 I published over forty short articles in *Sunset.* In addition, I have written shorts for *Northwest Travel, Buzzworm, Welcome Home, Real People, GRIT, Seattle Magazine, Travelin',* as well as fifteen parenting publications, regional newspapers, and local business publications. My successful experience writing short articles led me to create a workshop on writing shorts, which I have presented at a variety of regional writers' conferences. A positive response to my workshops led me to write this book.

I believe, and editors I have spoken with concur, that editors are more receptive to unfamiliar writers' queries on short articles than they are to feature-length article ideas. In this book I outline ways the editor and the writer benefit by starting their working relationship with short articles.

Taking the time to develop a positive working relationship with an editor can pay off in the long run. Show you can write dynamite short pieces and you'll gain the confidence of the editor. Once they know you can meet deadlines with accurate, well-written articles, selling feature stories will be much easier.

How I got started

My background is atypical for a writer. I did not write for school newspapers, nor plan a career that had anything to do with writing. Growing up, I never thought of writing as a career option. My only goal was to be a teacher.

Nevertheless, while studying for my degree and later teaching, I unknowingly prepared myself for my future writing career. First, I did extensive journaling; every day I typed pages of journal entries. If I was traveling, I took my electric typewriter along with me. When camping, I switched to a notepad. Writing was my way of processing the day. Without it, my day felt incomplete.

Second, because I was extremely shy, I spent many hours at parties and other social events sitting in a corner watching everything. On a subconscious level, this helped me develop the observation skills I now use in my writing.

My life as a professional writer began at age thirty-seven. I was staying home with my two young sons, ages five and two, when I spotted a small ad for a women's writing group welcoming moms and their kids to their monthly meetings. I had previously written short stories, solely for my own enjoyment, and thought this group would give me the incentive to pursue that kind of writing. The meetings sounded low-key and nonintimidating, so I decided to attend the next meeting. I showed up late, unshowered, and disorganized.

The meeting turned out to be a group of professional women writers with fax machines, editors, and deadlines. They not only took care of their daily grooming needs, they were organized enough to research and write articles on deadline, with children underfoot. Within moments I knew they had a lot to teach me, if only time management skills.

After attending meetings for three months, I felt the need for action. I was listening in on their writing adventures, but not writing a word myself. Without much thought to the outcome, I gave myself a deadline; before the next meeting, I had to contact an editor and at least try to write and publish an article.

Afraid of writing a query, I began my writing career by breaking the cardinal rule of writing: I called an editor — something all writers know is a no-no. I called the managing editor of *Northwest Baby & Child*, a free monthly publication put out by Baby Diaper Service. Experts tell novices to start submitting to a publication they know, and I knew this publication well. Every month I read it cover-to-cover.

Talking with the managing editor, I asked what topics she would be covering in the coming months. She mentioned nutrition and I knew that was for me; I wanted to write about my son, the picky eater. I got an okay to write an article on speculation (I would write the article, then she would decide if she wanted to buy it.)

Using my trusty electric typewriter, I wrote a rough draft at my dining room table. Although we had a computer in the house, I had never touched it; and I knew I couldn't learn to write and use a computer simultaneously. With a pair of scissors and a glue stick, I cut-and-pasted my second version together. This went on for several drafts, until I felt satisfied. Then I took it to a typist, who typed up my final draft.

The day my article was due, I drove my 350-word manuscript down to the editor's office. Sitting at a large table, working on that month's ad layout, she set my article aside and continued her work. Expecting an immediate response, I had to exercise maximum self-control and clamp my mouth shut to keep from screaming, "Look at it!" Somehow I managed to exit without making a scene.

Weeks later, I received a letter saying my article's publication date would be March 1989. An exciting moment, but nothing when compared to the day I held my published article. I was so thrilled I danced around the yard like an idiot. Not only did I get my first byline, I got a free month of diaper service as payment. I quickly learned bylines are addictive: the more I get, the more I want. Since that day in 1989, I have published 200 articles in forty national and regional publications.

Acknowledgments

My deepest appreciation goes to my husband Alan for his unwavering support and my sons, Spencer and Zander, who gave up weekends of fun so I could complete this book.

A heartfelt thank-you to my North by Northwest Writers' Club critique group, Helen McDonald, Karen McGeorge Sanders and Patti Piper, for years of support, writing tips, grammar checks, and a sustaining belief in my writing. With a special thank-you to Helen for the hours she spent proofreading this book.

A big thank-you to Nancy Thalia Reynolds, for suggesting I write this book, encouraging me along the way, and sharing her valuable copy editing skills.

I owe a debt of gratitude to Richards E. Bushnell, for teaching me the finer points of writing shorts.

"Good writing is a series of little things done well."

Chapter One
WHAT ARE SHORTS?

Why bother with shorts?

Shorts are articles that typically run 50 to 800 words in length. A few publications categorize 1,000 word articles as shorts. They can cover any subject, from travel to humor to health, and beyond. You'll usually find shorts towards the front of a magazine. Another name for a very short piece is filler.

Short articles give just enough information to pique a person's curiosity. These little articles give the essentials, such as why a particular event would be worth attending and when it's held, or three ways to organize your office and gain extra time. They don't hold out solutions to big problems or the finer points of an issue. To get the whole story, with details and expert opinions, the reader is usually directed to a phone number to call for more information. Readers can then use the short as a starting point and do some research on their own. (see appendix)

Strut your stuff

Editors look for writers who can provide their publication with a steady stream of good ideas, strong writing, and triple-checked facts. Demonstrate good writing skills and you have the possibility of receiving more assignments. If you show you are also pleasant to work with and know the importance of deadlines, you will have a good chance at steady work.

Many magazines prefer to start their working relationship with a new writer by assigning short pieces. Look through a copy of *Writer's Market* (see glossary). Under each magazine's listing there is a section called *Tips*. Here you'll find specific information on what publications are looking for from writers. In these sections, several magazines recommend that writers who want to break into their publication should start by proposing short article ideas.

Doable

No one would expect you to learn to swim by crossing the English Channel or try hiking by scaling Mount Everest. We learn new skills one step at a time. It takes many hours of practice to build-up endurance. You have to acquire a lot of specific skills, then learn to put them together. The same principle applies to writing. Instead of starting with a novel or 2,000-word feature article, try a bite-size project like a short article. You will learn all the skills needed for longer pieces and experience a sense of accomplishment for completing a writing project. This kind of short-term reinforcement should not be underrated; it can be euphoric.

Good money

There is good money in writing short pieces. I can earn twice as much money writing a 300-word article, without photos, for a large national magazine, than I can for a 1,200 word piece, with photos, for a regional publication.

Furthermore, national magazines usually pay my expenses and hire their own photographers to handle accompanying pictures. Working for regional publications I generally receive no additional money for expenses or required photographs. As inequitable as that sounds, there have been worse situations. When I wrote a 1,200-word article for a start-up magazine, with photos (including captions) and a sidebar of places to stay, local restaurants, and other attractions in the area, I was paid half what regional magazines pay, or a forth of what I get from national magazines for a shorter article. Of course, there are plenty of publications that pay in copies or nothing at all. If I have a personal need to write an article or want to donate it as a volunteer effort, I will consider writing for free. Otherwise, I want to be paid.

Why is there such disparity in pay? There can be several reasons. Many national magazines have an extensive advertising base and a large readership. Some regional magazines have the opposite situation: no advertisements and a small readership. Not that a publication with a strong advertising base will always pay well. Publications distributed for free generally pay less than subscription-based publications. The economic base of a magazine's readership also makes a difference (middle-class parents, single yuppies, or senior citizens). And don't forget arbitrary editorial decisions. I once received a moderate fee from a regional parenting magazine for first serial rights (see glossary) to a parenting article. A similar publication, in a different state, paid me two-thirds of the original fee for reprint rights (see glossary).

A well-written short article shows off your writing style, accuracy skills, and ability to meet deadlines. It also builds up your resume and book of clips (see glossary). If you get short articles published in national magazines, such as *Woman's Day* or *Eating Well*, you can include them in the list of places you've been published. You don't have to say it was only 250 words. Some people count having a letter published in the Letters to the Editor section, but I think that is stretching the truth too far.

Learn the inner workings of publications

From an editor's standpoint, assigning a short piece to a new writer (new to that publication, not necessarily new to writing) is less risky than assigning a feature article. With every assignment there is the possibility the writer will not match the magazine's style, miss the mark in content, or worse, miss the assigned deadline. If an article doesn't work out, the editor can be left with a gap in the magazine. The smaller the hole, the easier it is to fill.

The editor isn't the only one to benefit from this

arrangement. The editor learns about you and you learn an equal amount about the editor and publication. After you have an article published, ask yourself the following questions: Was your article published in a timely manner? Were you paid promptly? Did the published piece look like what you had written or was it edited beyond recognition? How you feel about the editing will depend on how well it was done. An edit that smoothes out rough transitions is worlds apart from a butcher job that twists paragraphs out of order.

Sometimes it is good to do more than one short for a publication before moving on to features. Years ago, I wrote two articles for a national environmental magazine. The first time I had a great experience, with lots of ongoing communication with the editor. We faxed revisions back and forth, and had several phone conversations about revisions to my article. Plus, the magazine paid me within thirty days of publication.

The next time I submitted a piece, there was no response. I waited the appropriate amount of time, probably three months, then wrote a letter asking about the status of my article. No response. Two months later I wrote again. No response. After waiting a bit longer, I called the editor. She never returned my call. Then, one day I was in a bookstore looking through a copy of the magazine and I found my article. I wrote again, this time asking for payment. No response. I tried every method I could think of to get my money, but the publication never paid me. I heard through another source that the publication was having financial problems; however, the editor never offered me any explanation.

A year later, a regional publishing house went through a period of financial adjustments, just after publishing one of my short articles. One of its publications folded and at the same time its postage rates changed. During this turmoil, the editor was good about writing letters explaining what was happening, why my payment was late, and when I could expect a check. The payment was late, but it eventually appeared in my mailbox. The editor's willingness to explain the situation, and pay me when she could, has kept me writing for the publication.

My experience with another national publication started off poorly. The first editor I worked with had very specific ideas on what he wanted. He liked big words and articles about "happening" places. Since I am not a "happening" person this caused a little bit of conflict.

Then the editor told me he wanted a certain take on my first assignment, a glass show. After talking with the artists and seeing samples of their work, I wrote up the story taking a different slant than the editor had requested. (Not a smart move on my part.) He ended up rewriting the article and giving himself the byline (see glossary). That's the bad news. The good news is I got the money.

While I wasn't happy about losing my byline, I liked the money enough to give it another go. By the time my next piece was due, I had a different editor. A short time later, I had another editor. This one stayed with me for quite a while. He not only helped me with articles I was working on for him, but worked with me to develop better writing skills.

One lesson I learned from this experience is: if you

don't get along with an editor try again later, there may be someone different doing the job.

The you-never-know factor

I am a strong believer in the you-never-know factor. You truly never know where something will lead. Through the years, I have seen what seemed like a small event in my life lead to bigger opportunities.

After writing numerous short articles on things to see around the Northwest, I felt quite knowledgeable in that area. Seeing a request for book writers to host an online chat for ExpressNet, a travel content area sponsored by American Express on America Online, I volunteered to do a show called "An Eclectic Tour of Seattle." I told them I did not have a book, but I did have lots of great ideas on things to see and do around Seattle. That one event had a wonderful domino effect.

In preparation for my show, I sat in on an online show Peggy van Hulsteyn was conducting, featuring her book, *The Birder's Guide to Bed and Breakfasts*. Her book was so interesting, I queried an editor saying I would like to review it. I got the go-ahead and wrote a review of *The Birder's Guide to Bed and Breakfasts* for a natural food store's monthly newsletter.

As publicity for my show, American Express sent press releases outlining who I was and what my show would cover to newspapers in my area. That netted me an article showcasing my past writing experience and my upcoming show in a local newspaper. This article led to a second article in another newspaper. Sharing this story and other experiences I have had with America Online at a North by Northwest Writer's Club meeting (a group of writers who meet in Lynnwood, Washington), resulted in a lengthy write-up in their monthly newsletter.

A story in *Byline Magazine May 95* offers another illustration of how far a short article can take you. Mary Ellen Brown's first published article was a short 250-word story about an experience she had with angels. After her story was published, the author of an "angel" book called to interview her. This led to Brown's experience with angels being re-enacted for a nationally televised documentary called *Angel Stories* and her name being listed in the credits.

Chapter Two
Market Research

Who buys shorts?

Browse through *Writer's Market* and you will find dozens of magazines that take shorts. Here is a partial list of publications and the topics for the short articles they generally publish:

Airline inflight publications—Business news, arts and entertainment, destinations, and restaurants.

Business magazines—New trends and outstanding entrepreneurs.

City magazines—What's happening around the city and nearby destinations.

Children's magazines—Animals, people, sports, and historical events.

Computer magazines—New software and electronic gizmos.

Food magazines—Food trends, new products, exercise, and restaurants.

Lifestyle magazines—Interesting people, food, and travel.

Parenting publications—Family travel destinations, advice, and how-to.

Travel magazines—Unusual places or unusual things to do in well-known places.

Reading through magazines you'll find ideas as well as markets for short articles. I found an article on strawbale houses in an airline magazine. Changing the slant, I interviewed owners of a strawbale construction company and sold the story to an environmental magazine.

Write what you like to read

This piece of advice has worked well for me. Most of my major successes have come from publications I know well and read regularly.

My first sale (see appendix), was with *Northwest Baby & Child*, a publication I received on a monthly basis with my son's cloth diapers, and read cover-to-cover. I knew its style and could fully relate to the subject—parenting.

Sunset is another magazine I know well; when I was growing up, my family always had a copy of *Sunset* on the coffee table. When I got married they gave me my own subscription. So in the early 90s, when I saw bylines in their Northwest Travel Guide, I knew there had been a change. I immediately wrote a letter to the Northwest Travel Guide editor saying, I had been reading *Sunset* since I was a kid, and I just noticed bylines for the first time. Did this mean I could submit ideas as a freelance writer? The editor called me and said "Yes, send me a list of ideas." I did some quick research and sent off four ideas. Within days, he gave me the go-ahead to write up one of my ideas.

Get the scoop on publications

Before you invest too much time preparing a query (see glossary) or even brainstorming ideas, write to the publication you are interested in and ask for copies of the following items:

Writer's guidelines—These give you basic information on what that specific magazine is looking for and which areas of the magazine are open to freelancers. The guidelines are usually general, but occasionally they add a zinger, something you really need to know.

Editorial calendar—This tells writers what topics the publication plans to cover during that calendar year, for which issue, and the deadline for proposing ideas. Under January, it might list four topics: filming movies outside Hollywood, traveling around Arizona, winter meals, and swimming, with a note at the bottom saying article proposals or queries are due by the first of November. Although this deadline is two months before publication, the editors usually have assigned writers long before then. Sitting under the sweltering summer sun is the best time for developing cool winter article ideas for most major magazines.

Timelines—A publication's timeline tells you when they plan each issue and when articles are due. Some publications are open to ideas one month before publication, while most work a minimum of two to three months ahead of schedule. A few magazines I work for plan their issues over a year in advance. If you want to submit a seasonal piece focusing on Valentine's Day, you need to know the magazine's deadline for February ideas. I got the go-ahead to write an article on gourmet chocolate in Seattle, for *Sunset*'s February issue, a year in advance. The deadline for the final manuscript was the first of August.

At the other end of the spectrum are local publications which accept new article ideas as few as three months in advance of publication, and whose deadlines are 30 days in advance of publication.

Annual index—This lists, by date, the topics the magazine covered in a given year. Not all publications have an index, but it is worth an inquiry. They are a wonderful time saver. With an index in hand, you can see if your idea was recently covered before you invest time composing a query.

If an idea was published over three years ago (you will need a series of indexes to determine this), it might be time to revisit the topic. A number of magazines, especially parenting magazines, are on three-year cycles. If a magazine published an article on the pros and cons of nursing babies, it will probably cover the same topic again, with a new slant, in three years, when there is a new crop of parents dealing with the issue.

To query or not to query—It is hard to know whether or not to write a query for a 200-word article. The query could easily be longer than the article you are proposing. Check for the magazine's preference in *Writer's Market* or in the publication's guidelines. Some magazines will not accept, or even look at, unsolicited manuscripts. In other words, if the editors did not ask it, they don't want to see it.

Tip—If you have a track record as a writer, or in the subject you want to cover, include a resume with your query, highlighting pertinent information.

Hunting and gathering

One of the questions most frequently asked of writers is "Where do you get your ideas?" The answer: everywhere. While not especially enlightening, it is true. Once you start looking for ideas, it is hard to turn off the potential-idea detector. Family and friends are always kidding me about turning everything we do into an article. Resources for starting your search include:

Newspapers—Look through local daily newspapers and weekly publications. Even browse through those horrid ones comprised mostly of ads. It only takes a sentence, or an interesting aside, to start a creative brainstorming session. You may not want to write about the stories you read, but something you see might stimulate other ideas you do want to pursue. I found one of my ideas for a national magazine in a "throw-away" paper. It took ten minutes to scan the paper and discover this article idea.

Magazines—For research purposes, don't limit yourself to the kinds of magazines you like reading. I found news about child development in a science magazine, a piece on food trends in an airline publication, and a travel idea in a business magazine.

Professional or social newsletters—These are good sources for new trends, gadgets, and cutting edge ideas.

Friends—Starting out, when I focused most of my writing on parenting issues, my rule of thumb was: if three people were talking about a topic, it was story material. Since switching my focus to travel, I pay rapt attention when friends mention a fun vacation spot or new restaurant. I try to restrain myself from asking too many questions, knowing how easy it is for me to turn into an interviewer instead of friendly listener. I make a point of getting the name and location, so I can follow-up on the lead.

Volunteer work—This is a great way to get an insider's view of a business. Along with hands-on experience, you will probably have access to newsletters and experts in the field to interview.

Internet—This world-wide shopping ground for topics of interest, and means of tracking down specific information, is a good place for locating experts for interviews; but be careful, get verification of interviewees' occupations and expert status before quoting them.

Contacts—Start recording names, phone numbers, addresses, and people's areas of expertise on a Rolodex.

InforTrac SearchBank—Available at some public libraries, this computerized search system holds a large data base of information on published articles. Type in an area of interest and the machine will list previously published articles on that topic, which magazine published them, the date of publication, and where the articles can be located. For example, if you type in a search on music therapy, you will learn which magazines have published articles about music therapy, the dates of publication, and if the library has access to those magazines. Once you have this information, you can see how many times the subject has been covered, and whether they used your slant.

These data banks are not only good for research, they can save you valuable time. When I put in a search on eyeglasses, I found the topic had been written about ad nauseam by every forty-year-old writer with new glasses. I could not think of any new slants, so I dropped the idea. A month later, I saw a review of a book with a new slant on this topic. It extolled the self-confidence needed for women to wear glasses instead of contact lenses.

Detective work

One of my favorite activities is taking a comment made during casual conversation and tracking down more information. If someone mentions a new hotel being built in Port Ludlow, I try to figure out who I could call for more information. For this search my first calls would be to the Port Ludlow Chamber of Commerce and the local Port Ludlow newspaper. Then I would try visitor information for the town or county or state.

Let's say you caught the last few minutes of a news broadcast saying something about a college back east that uses an experimental educational approach with children in elementary school. How do you find out the name of the college? You could try the following: call the television station where you heard the snippet, contact local and federal agencies that serve the educational community, or check with the education departments of local colleges.

The ability to track down information is essential for any kind of writing. Play around with this in your free time and you might dig up some interesting article ideas. Boldness also helps; learn to ask questions. Remember, you can ask anything. People may not answer, but you can ask.

Slanting ideas to the right market

As you read through the magazines you are targeting, pay attention to the language, sentence structure, and overall feeling or style. Is the language casual, academic, or sophisticated? Does the publication use quotations? Are there long narratives or descriptive sentences? Does it use quick snappy prose? Are bullets used to highlight key points? Are articles written in the first person or third person? Take notes. When you write an article for a particular publication, the editor will expect you to match the publication's style.

The ads will tell you a lot about a magazine's target audience. These are your readers, so you should pay attention, too. Advertisers are very careful where they place their ads. If you see an ad for a Mercedes, you can bet that a good share of the readers are wealthy enough to buy a Mercedes. This is not the place to pitch queries on penny pinching. On the other hand, a round-up piece on new gourmet kitchen gadgets or a luxury bed and breakfast might have a chance.

Once you have chosen your magazine, it is time to develop your slant. Make sure it is appropriate for the market you are targeting. For a coffee article in an environmental magazine, you could talk about chemicals used in growing non-organic coffee versus organic coffee. In a humorous article, the ubiquitous espresso stands in Seattle are fair game. A lifestyle magazine might want reviews of unique espresso cafés.

Read editorials in the front of magazines. These are "straight from the horse's mouth" information from editors telling you what they think is important. Letters to the editor give you more insight into the readers, while the selection of letters tells you about the editor.

No matter how old an idea is, if you can find a new slant, you've got a new story. And there is always a new slant. Take the joke about why the chicken crossed the road. I have heard this joke since elementary school, and people are still coming up with amusing new slants. Here is the latest rendition to come my way: "Do you know why the chicken crossed the road? To show the possum it is possible."

Chapter Three
Nuts and Bolts

How to write a query

Now that you have an idea, it is time to write a query letter. This is where you propose an article idea to a specific editor. Your job is to interest editors in your idea and tell them why you are the person to write this story. Using one of my favorite queries, "Stories Carved in Wood," I will give you an overview of how to write a query. I strongly recommend that you check out *How to Write Irresistible Query Letters* by Lisa Collier Cool (an excellent resource for learning how to write query letters), and *Writer's Market*, for more in-depth information.

Each query has three parts: an enticing first paragraph, a description of what your article will cover, and a statement about who you are. The whole thing should fit on one page.

The first paragraph, or lead, is of paramount importance. I got a clear picture of just how important when I spoke to Shannon O'Leary, Associate Editor for *Seattle Magazine*. I was interviewing her for "Write On," a radio show I co-produce for station KSER, in Lynnwood, Washington. Our topic was breaking into markets, and I was asking O'Leary what happens to a query after it arrives at her office.

She told me the post office delivers a mail crate full of queries to her office every week. To get through this volume of mail in a timely fashion, she peruses the first paragraph of each letter. If it doesn't catch her attention, she puts it in the rejection pile. This means you have a second to sell your piece. If a query warrants more attention, she puts it into a second pile, where it gets reread at a later date. That's where you want your letter to land.

For that to happen, you need a powerful lead paragraph, something that will spark the editor's interest. Check over the techniques described in Chapter Four in the section titled, "Draw people in," and read the accompanying query. These provide ideas on how to create good lead paragraphs.

The second section of your query tells the editor what your article will include. How long will your article be? This requires an estimated word count. If you already know which experts you will be interviewing (and if they have agreed to give you an interview) include their names and titles. What slant will your article have? Are you focusing on how someone does something, why they do it, how they got the idea to do it, or a hodgepodge of all three?

In the final section, tell the editor why you are the person to write the story. Do you have experience relating to your topic? Have you written on similar topics before? List other magazines that have published your articles; attach a resume, if it will help stress your qualifications.

Be sure you include a self-addressed stamped envelope (SASE) and copies of published articles or clips, if you have them. Many editors will not respond without a SASE. They will chuck your query into the trash unread.

Example:

Mr. Kerry A. Swagger
Editor
Successful Living!
Sycamore Avenue North
Eagerton, WA   90000-0000

November 10, 1991

Dear Mr. Swagger,

Searching through the evergreen forest in the Olympic Peninsula, David Boxley finds the perfect forty-foot cedar. With care the tree is downed and stripped of its bark. Cutting into the soft wood he uncovers the spirit which lives in the wood. Blending tradition with modern tools Boxley carves the cedar tree into a totem pole. Creating a story, the animals and figures become a library of myths and legends.

David Boxley is widely recognized as one of the leading Northwest Coast Indian carvers and artists. In the past fourteen years Boxley has created thirty-six totem poles. Currently he is working on a forty-foot Salmon Legend totem for Beaver Lake Park, in

Issaquah, Washington. The pole raising is set for the Fall of 1992.

I would like to propose an article, "Stories Carved in Wood," about David Boxley and the Salmon Legend totem he is creating. In this article I will explore Boxley's Alaskan Tsimshian tribal heritage, how he turns a tree into a storyteller, and the story behind the Salmon Legend totem. This article will run approximately 1,000 words and will include color slides. I would like to publish this article in time for interested readers to attend the pole raising.

My work has been published in 20 national and regional publications, including Mothering Magazine, Buzzworm, Seattle's Child, *and* RV West, *a regional travel magazine.* I have enclosed two published pieces as samples of my writing.

Sincerely,
Colleen Foye Bollen

Finding the puzzle pieces

Once you have gathered all your materials, you need to get your article down on paper. Since my method revolves around a computer, I am going to assume you have a computer or access to one.

Now is the time to get the information out of your head, off the scraps of paper you have collected, and into a computer. It helps me to think of the bits of research as a 500-piece puzzle. You have all the pieces there in the box; but you can't put it together from the box. You need to spread all the pieces out, try them in different spots, and see where they fit. Where are the edges? Is it a square puzzle or a triangular picture?

As you go through your research material look for the information that brings up the strongest images or the most important points. Have you ever put together a puzzle and had a piece or two that really brought the picture into focus? In an article these are the corner pieces — the pieces that illustrate the basic points: who, what, when, where, why, and how. Even shorts need these fundamental elements.

Don't forget your senses. The more senses (sight, smell, sounds, taste, and feeling—tactile and emotional—) you incorporate into your piece, the richer it will be. If you have a flair for it, and it's appropriate, a sense of humor also helps.

Be sure to triple check all facts. Before mailing your article, call your resource people and verify information. Some writers read quotes to their interviewees and get their okay. Ask people to spell their names and give their correct titles. Even a name as simple as Cindy Smith can be spelled numerous ways (e.g., Cyndi Smythe or Cindie Smyth). Don't forget to verify the correct spelling of the editor's name and title.

Asking the right questions

There may be times when you'll have to write about something that does not exist. This means creating something that is not quite fiction writing, but close.

I wrote about a glass exhibit before the artwork was made, and a brewery when it was just a cement floor and steel beams. I have written about powwows I haven't attended and chocolate I haven't tasted. While it is not essential that I see, experience, or taste the exact thing I am writing about, a foundation of knowledge about the subject is essential. I have seen lots of glass work, been to breweries, attended other powwows, and eaten pounds of gourmet chocolate. I have also learned to ask the right questions to people who have first-hand experience with the topic of my article. By the end of my interviews I should know how things look, feel, and smell. Sometimes people send me pictures or verbally paint me a picture of what I could expect to see. It usually takes interviews with more than one person to get the whole picture.

When writing a story about Northwest powwows, I asked one woman how I would locate the powwow once I got to town. She told me to follow the drum beats that vibrate through the ground. I used that image for my opening sentence, "Strong, steady drum beats pulsate through the ground and fill the air, calling visitors to the annual summer powwow."

Chapter Four
Secrets to Writing Short

Stay focused

I call this the hammer stage, when I pound my article into shape. I have my research, a lead, and interviews; now I have to figure out how I am going to get it all to flow together in a cohesive piece.

Sometimes it helps if I encapsulate what I am trying to say into one sentence. Other times an old-fashioned outline provides the structure for writing an article. I type the outline into the computer, then move information around until I have the major headings filled.

A newer method of outlining or brainstorming is "mapping." Using this technique you write a one-or-two-word title for the subject at the top of the page. Once you have done that, write other words or subjects related to the story randomly around the page. Draw lines connecting groups of ideas that seem to fit together, then rank them in importance. This should give you a framework for starting your piece.

A verbal approach I use for deciding on a direction for my story, or getting unstuck, is talking to a friend. (Be careful with this one and don't talk out the energy behind the article.) The idea is to briefly tell your friend about your story or trip.

Let's say I am writing a travel piece on Mount Rainier. I would call a friend and talk about the high points. Depending on my focus, these might be a description of a walk through a glacier field, the wildflowers and waterfalls we passed, or the inns and restaurants in the area.

As I talk about my trip, I make mental notes (sometimes written notes). Part of me observes what things I bring up, while another part asks myself—Are these the essential points I want to cover in my story? Occasionally, I don't know where I am going to go with a story until the words come out of my mouth. Then I pinpoint key elements by listening to what I tell my friend.

One of the most difficult parts of writing short is limiting what you say. You may have gone to the best restaurant in the world while traveling to your destination, but if it doesn't fit into your word count, you can't mention it. File away the information and hope, at a later date, you can write a review of the restaurant.

Here are some basic figures to help you plan out your article and determine how much room you have for each main point. Typically, a sentence runs about twelve to fifteen words and a paragraph has four to five sentences. If you are writing a 300-word article, this means you can include four main paragraphs made up of five sentences each. Not much room, but you'll be surprised how much information you can wrangle into that tiny space.

I once read, "The sentences you most love are the ones to cut," a piece of advice I had every intention of ignoring. Then I noticed how often my cute comments or unique observations broke the flow of my article. Seventy-five percent of the time, I now cut my favorite sentences from the final manuscript.

First draft, second draft, third draft and more

Once you know your main points, it's time to turn off your internal editor (easier said than done) and start writing. Your first draft will be bad. Count on it, but don't worry about it. Just write. You will have plenty of time to revise and edit later. Right now you need to get the main points down on paper. The purpose of the first draft is to get you past the research/thinking stage and into writing. Ninety percent of writing is rewriting, so just put something down on paper. Try to include who, what, when, where, why, and how.

Editing this first draft takes a strong ego. It is not unusual to hate three-quarters of what you've written. Instead of focusing on the lame parts, look at the one-quarter of good stuff. This is what you will build on in the second draft.

Using a computer makes tweaking a manuscript easy, I couldn't begin to tell you how many rewrites I do per article. Once I have the main text on my computer, I keep reworking minor points until it sounds right. You read me correctly, I said sounds, not looks, right. I read it out loud to myself and anyone else who will listen. This helps me find muddled sentences and awkward transitions. [Note: Reading out loud is done in addition to fine-comb editing, not in place of this essential step.]

Before mailing the final copy to an editor I have someone else read over the manuscript. It is amazing what I miss when editing my own manuscript. Being too familiar blinds me to missing commas, the overuse of certain words, and typos.

Draw people in

The sad truth is that you have one second to draw readers into your article. The lead has to capture their attention and pull them on to the next paragraph and the next. This means you need a strong lead paragraph, something that will hook people into your article as they thumb through the magazine.

There are many kinds of leads. Here are some samples of the more popular types:

Bold

• Jerry Camarillo Dunn, Jr. (*National Geographic Traveler*, July/August 96) wrote this bold lead, "If your idea of a good time is plunging toward pavement from hundreds of feet in the air, or zipping around 360-degree loops with enough G-force to give you a temporary face-lift, you'll enjoy celebrating the International Year of the Roller Coaster."

- In just 56 words, Laurie Lico Albanese (*Mothering Magazine*, Spring 94, Issue 17) tells readers how a delicious summer night turned into a hellish experience. "On a beautiful summer night three years ago, I was sitting on my back porch when a woman in a nearby apartment building began shrieking, 'Stop! Please stop!' Her cries were followed by the deep, angry voice of a man grunting and shouting unintelligibly. I waited a few seconds, frozen in place, straining to hear more."
- I wrote this lead for Swedish Medical Center in the Fall of 94: "If pain is the first thing that hits you when you wake up each morning and the last thing you cope with when going to bed at night, here is some news for you. Pain is not a necessary consequence of an old injury or long-term disease; chronic pain can be treated."

Every time I read this quote during a writing workshop, people come up to me afterwards to find out more about easing their pain. Because pain is a horrible thing to deal with on a daily basis, this lead elicits an immediate response. By starting the article with this sentence I attract the attention of people interested in resolving pain issues for themselves, friends, and family members.

Question

- For my article "Turn Exercise into a Healthy Habit" (*PCC Sound Consumer*, February 94), I wrote this lead; "What's the first thing that comes to mind when you hear the word exercise? If you are among the sixty-six percent of Americans who have resisted joining the fitness craze it might be a little five-letter word, g-u-i-l-t. A small word packed with emotion."

Statistics

• Writing about the Naval Undersea Museum, Kraylen Kelly (*Northwest Travel*, December 95) began with this lead, "More than two-thirds of the earth's surface is ocean, but we know far less about our undersea than we do of the dark side of the moon according to Bill Galvani, director of the Naval Undersea Museum at Keyport, Washington."

One reason I like this lead is because it's so different from the slant I took when writing about the same museum. Here is my lead (*Sunset*, January 95), "Trieste II sits in the parking lot looking more like a tipped over milk bottle than a bathyscaphe capable of diving to a depth of 20,000 feet under the sea. It's the first of many strange-looking vehicles you'll see while exploring the Naval Undersea Museum, which opened to the public in 1991 to showcase the U.S. Navy's achievements in underwater discovery, rescue, and warfare."

• For The Mountaineers, August 94, I wrote, "Snoqualmie Falls is the second largest tourist attraction, in Washington state. (Mount Rainier is the first.) Popularized by the `Twin Peaks' television series, the Falls are known around the world. Yet most of the 1.5 million tourists visiting Snoqualmie Falls annually don't realize the falls are a managed phenomenon — less than seven percent of the natural flow cascades over the 268-foot cliff."

Folklore

• Providence Cicero (*Seattle Magazine*, March 95) paraphrases an old saying in this lead: "An old Japanese saying holds that by eating something pleasant that you have never tasted before, you lengthen your life by 75 days. If that's the case, regular visits to Seattle's International District could make us all nonagenarians."

• I gave *The Three Little Pigs* a new twist (*Buzzworm*, January 93) with this lead: "The big, bad wolf may have blown down the little pig's straw house, but straw-bale homes have been known to stand up to tornadoes." (see appendix)

Play on words

• Karen McGeorge Sanders (*Llama's Magazine*, January/February 95) wrote, "A llama a day keeps the doctor paid," in a story about a hospital using llamas for a local fundraiser.

• Doing a story about gourmet chocolate shops in Seattle (*Sunset*, February 96) I wrote, "On a recent pilgrimage to Fran's Chocolates, the storefront was packed tighter than a box of truffles."

Descriptive

• I started a travel story (*Sunset*, September 95) this way, "From the outside our tepee glowed like a Japanese lantern. Inside a campfire flickered at the center of the tepee. Smoke drifted up and out the flaps at the peak of the lodgepoles."

Whatever the editor requests

Sometimes editors have specific ways they want writers to start an article. When I was writing a story about the Mystery Cafe, in downtown Seattle, my *Sunset* editor told me to write it as a mystery. With that idea in mind, I developed this lead: "Bring cash," said the voice on the phone, "and arrive before 8 P.M." With mild trepidation, we followed the mysterious voice's directions to a deserted store. An operative disguised as a waiter directed us to the cafe." (*Sunset*, March 95)

A few months later I was working on an article about trout farms. My son Spencer and I headed out on our first fishing adventure, void of practical knowledge. It didn't faze me that we knew nothing about fishing; I figured we'd learn as we went along. At the trout farm they gave us each a bamboo pole and bait and showed us how to put the two together. I hoped to learn the rest from watching people down at the pond. Two things went wrong with this plan; first, there was no one else down at the pond, and second, we caught a fish right away. There we stood with a fish hanging on the line and no idea how to get it unhooked.

My *Sunset* editor wanted me to write about trout farms using first person. I produced this lead, "I got one," yelled my son, Spencer. "What do I do now?" That question hung helplessly in the air next to a wiggling trout. With only five minutes of angling experience between mother and son, our knowledge was limited to baiting the hook." (*Sunset*, July 95)

Cooking it down

This is where you cut to the quick; get rid of unnecessary words, and strengthen what is left. Use an active voice and strong verbs; adjectives tend to gum up an article's flow.

Think of it as simmering soup: the longer you cook it, the more liquid will evaporate, and the stronger the broth will become. The part that evaporates is the non-essential part. It was necessary to start with it, but you don't need it in the final product.

If the image of cooking doesn't fit, you can try pruning or sculpting. Prune a tree and you give it shape — and it bears better fruit. When sculpting, you take away non-essential clay to create the work of art. Both analogies also apply to writing.

As you cook, prune, or sculpt your article, go back over your outline or list of key points. Have you covered the important points? If your word count is too high, look over your piece and see if there is any superfluous information. Remember, writing short means staying focused on a small piece of the story.

Review the information you learned when researching markets. Check the sentence length. Does the magazine for which you are writing this article use short or long sentences? Is its tone casual or sophisticated? Does it use quotes or flowery descriptions? Pull out your background information, a copy of the publication's writer's guidelines, and a copy of the magazine. As you rewrite your article follow any directions the editor has given you and match the magazine's style as closely as possible.

Chapter Five
Final Touches

Ways to shorten phrases

As you begin writing short articles, you'll learn ways to automatically shorten phrases. Here are a few of my standard condensing techniques:

• Use bullets to relieve the monotony of solid text and save words.

• Only include quotes that add something special.

• Use strong nouns and verbs, fewer adverbs and adjectives.

• Use an active voice.

• Study poetry, it is the master of condensed language.

• Collect common ways to shorten stock phases, such as:

The admission is = Admission costs

The store is open from 8 AM to 5 PM = Hours are

have to = must
looks like = resembles
after that = subsequently

Manuscript preparation

On page one, in the upper left hand corner, type your name, address, phone number, and Social Security Number. If you have them, include your fax number and E-mail address. In the upper right hand corner, put the word count (most computers have a word counter built-in), the rights (see glossary) you are offering for sale and your copyright notice (see glossary). This should all be single-spaced.

Center the title one-third of the way down the page. Drop down four lines and begin typing your manuscript, double-spaced. Use standard paragraph indentations: one tab or five spaces. Margins should be one and a half inches on all sides of the page. On every page after the first, type your last name, the article's working title and the page number along the bottom of the page. The second page of your manuscript would read: Bollen—Shorts: A Gateway Into New Markets—2. (see appendix) When your manuscript is ready to mail, enclose a self-addressed stamped envelope with the correct postage.

Ouch, that hurts

A lover's rejection might be hard to accept, but once spoken, you know where you stand. A pink slip from work means you are losing your job, pure and simple. What's not clear are the obtuse rejection letters writers receive. In the publishing world rejections come in so many forms I have often thought there should be a rejection interpretation class to decipher editors' messages. For lack of standardized guidelines, I have developed my own decoding system.

The quarter piece of paper, photocopied so many times the cryptic message is difficult to read, receives my worst rating. *"Dear Contributor: We regret your query/article does not meet our current editorial needs. The Editors."* Between "Dear Contributor" and "The Editors," there isn't an inkling of personal communication or a clue telling me why my query/article was rejected. I've decided, if my rejection isn't worth a whole piece of paper or a real person's signature, it's time to look for a new market. My environmentally aware self appreciates the paper saving, but my ego feels shortchanged.

The same type of form letter, on a whole sheet of paper, signals a slight degree of caring. Although I still struck out, my submission was worthy of a whole-page reply, and if I lucked out, a real person scrawled their signature at the bottom.

Then there's the multiple-choice letter with the appropriate box checked next to the reason for rejecting my masterpiece. Reasons for rejection might include: duplicates similar material on file; focus is too narrow; subject is too broad; article is not timely; it's just not us; and of course, it does not meet our editorial needs. Multiple-choice letters give me a clue why my submission was rejected. It could have been a good idea poorly timed, or maybe I misunderstood the publication's focus. Generally, I'll keep these magazines on my submit-to list.

After dozens of form-letter rejections, it's refreshing to receive a personalized reply, with my name, my article's title, a brief note, and a personal signature. The minute or two it took to write that note is repaid by my overwhelming appreciation and new article ideas. These folks earn my top rating.

Rejection letters praising my submission, "it's wonderful, funny, well-crafted ...," cause mixed emotions. They're saying I did everything right, and they still aren't going to buy my work. It reminds me of high school dates that ended with, "you're a nice person, but ..."

Poet Emily Warn once told me that she averages fifteen rejections per poem before she gets an acceptance. Embracing this philosophy, she cheers each rejection, because it brings her poem closer to publication.

A rule from my yet-to-be written writer's code book, states "For every twelve queries in circulation, at least one will succeed." According to this theory, for every acceptance there are eleven possible rejections. Not great odds. Strict adherence to this rule could quickly qualify any writer for an advanced degree in rejection interpretation; where an honorary graduate gets to choose between five rolls of rejection-slip wallpaper or a year's supply of ego-sized bandages.

No response

While rejection can be hard to accept, an editor's failure to respond at all is even harder to take. After you have mailed your query/article, waited the allotted time (check *Writer's Market* for specific magazines' response times and add a month), and still received no response, it's time for action. Some publications have a policy of not responding to queries on shorts; this tidbit of information should be in the writer's guidelines. If the publication does not have this policy, write a letter politely requesting the status of your query/article. Towards the end of your letter say, in the nicest words possible, that you would like a response by (give a specific date, usually a month away), and if you don't receive a response by then, the publication can consider your submission withdrawn. If this deadline passes without a response, give yourself a day to wallow in the writer's plight, then mail the piece out to another magazine. The only way your ideas will be published is if you keep them circulating until they are bought.

Learning from bad experiences

Most interactions with editors or publications hold lessons to be learned. Sometimes it is a red neon sign blinking AVOID, AVOID, AVOID. Other times it is a lesson you can apply to interactions with new publications. I have had several lousy things happen to published manuscripts, including withheld byline, another person's name under my article, and the misspelling of my name. The worst experience was when I submitted an article to one magazine and the article came out in its sister-publication.

Before writing my article, I studied an issue of the first magazine in minute detail. I meticulously matched its style, sentence length, and lines of quotations. Then the published article came out in a different publication — a magazine I had never heard of, much less read. Worst of all, every word I had painstakingly written was altered. My beginning was at the end and my end was at the beginning. The only recognizable parts were the quotes. The final copy was so different from my version and my style of writing that I couldn't use it as a clip. My only consolation was good money, paid on time.

While I liked being well paid, it didn't make what the publication did right. I wrote to the editor, expressing my displeasure. I told him, as a professional writer I would have liked the opportunity to rewrite the article or make changes he wanted. I never received a response from him. Needless to say, I never submitted another query to either publication.

Knowing that every experience holds lessons, I scoured the depths of this exchange and learned the importance of asking for the right to preview an article before publication. I don't always get it, but it doesn't hurt to ask.

Chapter Six
NOW THAT YOU ARE PUBLISHED

Market yourself

After you have written and published a couple of short articles for a magazine, it's time to query on a longer piece. Use the same query techniques discussed earlier, starting off with a dynamite lead. In the closing paragraph, tell the editor which of your articles he has previously published. Yes, we all think they should know, but editors work with many different writers, so why take the chance. Editors also quit, or are replaced without notice, and someone new may be reading your article idea.

The number of short articles you need to have published before making the jump from short to long articles varies from magazine to magazine. If you don't get into features right away, keep writing strong short pieces and bide your time. Persistence, exceptional ideas, and good writing are the keys.

Another option is to use your short articles to break into different publications. First-class shorts, published in prestigious magazines, make great stepping stones into other publications. Use them as clips when you query on new ideas and when asking to write a long article based on a previously published short article. A well-known magazine is a great addition to your resume and list of credits. Feature articles are not necessarily the final goal. Some writers are happy writing shorts and use their condensing skills as a gateway into technical writing.

Writing for CD-ROMs

Not only do some publications pay good money for shorts, writing shorts can lead to high paying positions in the field of technical writing. During a discussion with Peg Cheirett, founder and president of Wasser, Inc. (a temporary employment agency that places writers and editors in technical jobs in the Puget Sound area), I learned about an interesting way to build on a career of writing shorts. She said producers of CD-ROMs look for journalists with a track record of writing short concise pieces. The proliferation of these markets signals more work opportunities for writers who can condense bodies of material, while keeping the writing snappy and entertaining. Temporary agencies offer a good way to get your foot in the door. Once you have credits working in this field, it will be easier to get other work with or without an agency.

Greeting cards

If you are good at thinking up pithy sayings, you can make good money writing greeting cards. Companies pay between $25 and $150 per card or sentiment.

This market is booming. In fact, fifty percent of all first-class mail is greeting cards. On average, each person receives thirty-one greeting cards a year. Card racks at your local supermarket or variety store are good places to familiarize yourself with differences among lines of cards and get a feel for what is selling. For a listing of greeting card company addresses and general needs, check the latest *Writer's Market*.

Using the leftovers

Shorts don't have to be one-shot articles. Here are some ideas on how to expand and resell them:

• Use a short as the springboard for a feature article. Shorts can always be expanded. You've already done the legwork, gathered research, and figured out the key points. Besides, turning it into a feature gives you a chance to put back all the good stuff you had to cut. Another way to lengthen a short article is by adding snazzy quotes or doing a round-up of similar pieces.

• If you find yourself writing several shorts on one theme, think about combining them into a book. For example, a selection of travel shorts can be transformed into a guidebook, with each event and/or outing given one page and a photo.

- Find a new angle or slant for your story and create a new piece. After writing a story about a Native American carver who works with his young son, I turned the story around and wrote it from the son's perspective.
- Take the easy road and sell it as a reprint. If you can avoid selling any one publication all rights, you can resell your piece over and over. Be sure you let each publication know it is buying reprint rights, not only is it the honest thing to do, it is the right thing to do.

Chapter Seven
Precious Nuggets

Ask editors for input

Once you have established a relationship with an editor, ask for suggestions on how you can improve your work. Be prepared to hear the truth. Just because he or she is publishing your work doesn't mean there is no room for improvement. I have had editors tell me some pretty ego-damaging things. One editor said the reason he started working with me was because he liked my ideas, not my writing. Another editor said my writing was flat. The worst was when an editor who had once praised my work, saying it was exactly what he wanted from writers, told me he didn't have time to help me fix all my mistakes. (Ouch, that hurt.)

With each editor, I listened, took notes and kept my mouth shut. Politely thanking them for their input, I gently hung up the phone and s-c-r-e-a-m-e-d. After ranting about the wrongness of their opinion and adamantly defending myself, I pulled out my notes and reread what they had said. Tiny grains of truth shone through my bruised ego. Putting their input to work in my next assignment, I have always seen improvements in my work.

If you are going to ask the editor's opinion, you need to have an open mind and closed mouth. This is no time for "yes-buts," or explanations; put a silencer on your automatic self-defense system. This exercise will help toughen up your ego and tighten your writing. Take notes and say thank you. If the words were too harsh, put your notes away until the sting dies down. Once you have regained your ego, take a peek.

Support groups

I was lucky to start my writing career in the bosom of a very supportive and knowledgeable group of women. There aren't enough glowing words to describe all the ways they helped me learn the trade. When that group disbanded, I set out to find a new group.

After visiting several writing clubs in the area, I joined North by Northwest Writer's Club. My quest for a new critique group (see glossary) was answered at my first meeting; a non-fiction critique group was just starting up and I jumped onboard.

My critique group has been meeting once a month for

six years. During this time we have developed non-threatening ways to review each other's manuscripts. Our number-one rule is that the writer gets the last say. We give editing ideas on manuscripts and the writer decides if she wants to incorporate those ideas or let them slide. Second, we always state things in a positive way, such as: "you might think about adding more description", "what would happen if you incorporated the strategy you used in your article about bears into this piece", or "tell me what you most want readers to know about this subject." The group also shares information on editors, publications looking for new writers, and upcoming contests. We have even found each other writing assignments. Best of all, my critique group offers support during down times, praise for accomplishments, and valuable hard-earned advice.

Writer's block

Many writers have trouble with writer's block, or at least writer's stop signs. They are writing away on an article, when all of a sudden they come to an abrupt stop. At this juncture there are several things they can do.

Irving Stone was once quoted as saying, "When I have trouble writing I step out of my studio into my garden and pick weeds until my mind clears. I find weeding to be the best therapy there is for writer's block."

For me, swimming does the job. The monotony of swimming back and forth, back and forth, is almost meditative. My technical mind is busy keeping me from drowning, while my creative mind is free to work out solutions to problems or ways to create transitions.

The following ideas may help you unblock your creative energy:

- Read books on writing such as *bird by bird* by Ann Lamont, *Wild Mind* and *Writing Down the Bones* by Natalie Goldberg, or *Artist's Way* by Julia Cameron.
- Try a change of scene, a day trip; anything to break up patterns that are restricting you.
- Read biographies; look at the lives of others. Sometimes reading success stories helps a person become reoriented and motivated.
- Try to keep two or three projects going at once — all with different emotional tones. If you can dance back and forth between a funny story, a sad story, a research piece, and perhaps even a poem, you won't find yourself getting burned out on one emotional tone or project.
- Physical exercise provides an infusion of air into the stomach, gets the blood flowing, and the creative juices going.
- Change the time of day you write.
- Listen to different kinds of music while you work.

Dream on

There is a lot more to dreaming than fantasizing about fame and fortune. Dreams can give you concrete help with your writing.

In the book *Writers Dreaming*, published by Crown/Carol Southern Books in 1994 and by Vintage in 1995, author Naomi Epel recounts numerous ways successful writers have used their dreams in their work. The book is the result of Epel's work with dreams and her job as a literary escort. Assigned the task of escorting writers promoting their books in Northern California, she often had writers, tired of talking about their owns lives, ask her about her life. When she mentioned her work teaching dreamwork classes, they frequently perked up with interest. Over time, she realized there was material for a book in what she was hearing about creativity, writing, and dreams.

In the book, Maya Angelou is quoted as saying, "There is a dream which I delight in and long for when I'm writing. It means to me that the work is going well. Or will go well." She later adds: "And then there are terrifying dreams when the work is really going badly. I don't even want to talk about them. It gives them too much power."

Sue Grafton, author of the alphabet mystery series, declares, "a frightening dream is wonderful for me because it recreates all the physiology that I need in describing my private-eye heroine, Kinsey Millhone, in a dangerous situation."

It probably won't surprise you to learn that Stephen King uses his nightmares in his books. While writing one book he says, "I woke up and I was very frightened. But I was also very happy. Because then I knew what was going to happen. I just took the dream as it was and put it in the book. Dropped it in. I didn't change a thing."

For me, dreams have provided numerous solutions to sticky problems. When I am having difficulty writing an article I find it helpful to sleep on the problem. Before going to bed I ask my subconscious to help me develop the right slant or a good closing paragraph. As I sleep my subconscious mind takes over and I often wake up with a solution to my problem. Some people get more out of this exercise when they write down a specific, open-ended question that pertains to the problem they are trying to resolve.

Two key parts of this exercise are thinking about the question as you drift off to sleep and putting a notebook by your bed to record the dream when you first wake-up. A tape recorder can also be used to catch dreams.

In his book *Where People Fly and Water Runs Uphill: Using Dreams to Tap The Wisdom of the Unconscious* author Jeremy Taylor says, "The thoughts and feelings we casually entertain while falling asleep always exert a strong influence on the dreams that follow." By holding onto a conscious thought while falling asleep, you can use the power of dreams to enhance your writing.

Writing exercises

These exercises were designed as practice tools. If you can complete them to your satisfaction, it's time to start sending out queries on a short article.

- Using just 500 words, describe last year from your personal point of view. Sound impossible? Try it. You may find yourself screaming, "It can't be done!" In a sense that's true. You can't say everything that happened. There is only room for the highlights, probably the top five events. Some important things are bound to get cut, and that's the tough part. The idea is to focus on the essence of last year.

- In 300 words, write about your town's main attraction. Give enough information to activate a reader's curiosity. Write down things that would make readers want to jump in their car and go see it for themselves.

- Using only 300 words, write about your most embarrassing moment. What happened? How did people around you respond? What went on inside of you?

- You have 250 words; write the story behind your name. Does it involve family history, literature, or a famous person? If you don't have a good true story, make one up.
- Limiting yourself to 400 words, describe a turning point in your life. When did it happen? Were you instrumental in creating this event or was there an outside impetus at work?

When all is said and done

I have shared what I know on writing shorts in the hope that it will shorten your road to success. Writing is one of the few occupations in which we train our competition, an unusual quirk I am proud to bolster. I wish you well on your adventure with writing. It takes a lot of hard work, a tough skin, and stick-to-itiveness to be a writer. I would love to hear your comments and stories of your successes.

Best of luck.

>Colleen Foye Bollen
>PO Box 77598
>Seattle, WA 98177
>E-mail CBollen@AOL.com

Glossary

Byline—The author's name at beginning or end of a published article.

Clips—This refers to photocopies or clippings of articles you have published. Tearsheets are original copies of your articles, "torn" from a publication.

Copyright—The copyright law protects a writer's original work. It states that you own the copyright to publish and benefit from anything you write, from the moment it is written. When submitting your work to a publication, you may affix the copyright symbol ©, the year, and your name. This creates a copyright notice, © 1996 Colleen Foye Bollen.

Critique—A review or evaluation of your work.

Query—A one-page letter telling the editor about the article you want to write, and why you are the person to write the article.

Reprints—These are previously published articles, originally sold with one time rights or first North American serial rights. Publications usually pay half to a quarter of the original fee for reprint rights.

Rights—When you sell your work to a publication, you are giving the publisher the right to use your work in one or more ways. The type of right sold spells out how a publication can use the article.

First serial rights—The publication buys the right to be the first publication to publish the article. You retain the copyright and can sell it as a reprint. The qualifier "North American" specifies a geographical limit to the license.

One time rights—The publication buys non-exclusive rights to publish the article in its circulation area. The piece can be published simultaneously by another magazine with a different circulation area.

All rights—The title says it all; the publication acquires exclusive and total rights to your article. You cannot sell this article again. Basically, you are selling the copyright to the article.

Writer's Market—A book filled with information on over 4,000 places to sell your articles. It is revised yearly, so look for the latest edition.

APPENDIX

Here are samples of short articles I have written. Each piece showcases a different form of writing: personal essay, travel, environmental, business profile, and restaurant review.

Personal experience
My first published article, originally published in Northwest Baby & Child, *March 1989.*

Colleen Foye Bollen 330 words
PO Box 77598 First North American Serial Rights
Seattle, WA 98177
(206) XXX-XXXX
SSN XXX-XX-XXXX
FAX (206) XXX-XXXX
E-Mail CBollen@AOL.com
© 1989 Colleen Foye Bollen

Eating My Words

When my first son, Zander, was born I was determined to serve him well-balanced meals. After all, I had taught preschool for over eight years. Surely I knew all about children and food. I still remember those days, before motherhood, when I knew so much. I was a self-professed expert on children.

Little did I suspect that Zander had a say in what he ate. Nor did I guess that I'd been blessed with a picky eater. Zander ate so little, I wasn't sure what kept him growing. According to my calculations, he should have been malnourished and scrawny. As it was, Zander was a big healthy-looking boy. The doctor's chart said he was doing fine. But I knew in my heart he was not getting the right nourishment.

I spent hours creating nutritional meals. I made casseroles by the dozen, hiding soy and wheat germ in them. I filled ice cube trays with fresh pureed vegetables. Zander would not eat any of it. No suggestion for adding nutrition to Zander's diet was ignored. Still he continued to dismiss my efforts with a turn of his head or a "yuck." He had no regard for my hours of labor. When I did manage to get a bite into his mouth, it was usually returned with a raspberry in my face. He unilaterally refused my nutritional masterpieces.

The list of foods Zander would not eat grew faster than he did. No amount of coaxing or "flying airplane" spoons would pry his mouth open. I was amazed at the guilt I felt. I kept thinking I should be able to do something.

After months of worry, mountains of guilt, and several trips to the doctor for reassurance, I decided to change tactics. I started giving Zander multi-vitamins and accepted what I could not change anyway. I maintained my nutritional standards where I could, but my ideals faded in the face of reality. I threw my theories away and ate my words. "Yuck".

Travel
333 words
Unpublished

Ross Dam's Fall Tour

Buildings shrink to doll-size proportion and glacier peaks gain grandeur as the Incline Railroad Lift ascends 558-feet up Sourdough Mountain. Once used to transport rail cars to the Diablo Dam construction site, the lift now carries Ross Dam tour groups.

At the top, the tour follows the railroad bed one third of a mile to the boat landing. Walk, or catch a ride in the van; either way, the views of Diablo Dam and the North Cascade mountain range are spectacular.

Step aboard Alice Ross III, a 45-foot tour boat, and enjoy a relaxing half-hour ride across Diablo Lake, through steep canyon walls lined with evergreens and a sprinkling of colorful deciduous trees.

Arriving at the Ross Powerhouse, the picture postcard scenery disappears as you enter a dim concrete tunnel. Follow the low, rumbling sound to the roar of hydroelectric turbines, straight through the heart of a large generator.

Climb twenty-two stairs to the outdoor observation area. Here you can view Ross Dam, the largest dam on the Skagit project. Completed almost a quarter of a century before the North Cascades Highway was built, this 540-foot dam is a testimony to the workers' ingenuity and fortitude.

A quick look inside the Control Room reveals walls covered with a mass of dials, gadgets, and levers. Dwarfed by the equipment, a sole operator monitors the automated powerhouse from a computer station at the center of the room.

After a return boat trip and ride down the Incline Lift, it's time for the final segment of the tour, an all-you-can-eat chicken and vegetarian spaghetti dinner in the Diablo Cookhouse.

Seattle City Light's Skagit Hydroelectric Project Fall Tours run once a day from 11 A.M. to 3 P.M. from Saturday and Sunday, September 1 through 29. Wheelchair accessibility is limited. Tours cost $25 for adults 12 and over; $22 for seniors over 62; $12.50 for youths ages 6 through 11; free for kids 5 and under. Reservations are strongly recommended. For information call Skagit Tours (206) 233-2709.

Environmental
303 words
Originally published in Buzzworm, *January/February 1993*

Straw-Bale Houses

The big, bad, wolf may have blown down the little pig's straw house, but straw-bale homes have been known to stand-up to tornados.

Straw-bale construction appears to have sprung up in the Sand Hills of Nebraska in the late 1800s. Once popular with homesteaders, this unusual technique is getting a second look. Many people are drawn to the low cost, ease of construction, high insulation value, and the fact that—

unlike wood structures—it uses an annually renewable resource, straw.

From the time Matts Myhrman and Judy Knox saw their first straw-bale house, it was love at first sight. After researching straw-bale structures in Nebraska, they founded, "Out On Bale," a clearinghouse providing resources and support for straw-bale construction projects.

There are two approaches to building with straw bales. The first technique uses straw-bales to form weight bearing walls. Bales are laid like giant bricks on a foundation and pinned with metal or wooden rods. Walls are then covered, with plaster or stucco.

The second method uses straw bales as insulation for framed or post and beam houses. According to Myhrman, "This version is actually not a straw-bale house; it is a straw insulation house. If you use fiberglass insulation you don't call it a fiberglass house."

"Plastered straw-bale construction creates long lasting housing. If built properly and maintained, straw-bale structures can have a useful life span of at least 90 years," explains Myhrman. "The oldest existing straw house I know of was built in 1914, in northern Nebraska, and it's still occupied."

Bale buildings are extremely fire resistant. Tightly baled straw smolders, but does not burn quickly. As long as the bales are covered with stucco, plaster, aluminum siding or sheetrock there is little danger of fire.

For information on straw-bale houses, contact Out on Bale at 1037 East Linden Street, Tucson, AZ 85719, (602) 624-1673.

Business profile
681 words
Originally published in PCC Sound Consumer, *April 1995*

Kalani Organica Coffee and Teas

Many people would say starting a coffee company in Seattle is like seeding the clouds over a rain forest. With so many local companies, why start another? It wasn't steel nerves that gave Karen Gorder and Constance Neely the confidence to start Kalani Organica, a certified organic coffee and tea company. "We were naive," says Karen, "And I think that's good. We didn't know anything about the coffee business. Now we know Seattle is the most competitive city in the world in which to start a coffee company. Getting people to switch coffees is a challenge, but we have a unique niche."

- **Twists of Fate**

Sipping a cup of just-roasted-yesterday espresso, I talked with Karen Gorder about the genesis of Kalani.

Karen, a self-described professional student, pursued many occupations before starting Kalani. Moving through various fields of study, she gained the skills necessary to run a successful coffee company. Several unexpected twists of fate brought Karen to this point. In fact, she hadn't intended to start an organic coffee company at all. Three years ago, when Karen decided to open a cafe and serve organic coffee, she couldn't find any that tasted good. So, she decided to roast her own.

Layers of experience made this seemingly daunting

task, doable. Weaving together knowledge she gained earning degrees in horticulture and art design, and experience running other businesses, Karen came up with the right blend of skills for producing coffee. Constance Neely filled out the joint resume with a Ph.D. in Agro-ecology and numerous connections with organic farmers around the world.

Kalani products are all-organic. That means the coffee, teas and spices are grown free of manufactured chemical-pesticides, herbicides and commercial fertilizers. The products not only promote environmentally sound ideals, they taste great. If you haven't tried organic coffee lately, you are in for a treat. Unlike the turpentine-flavored organic blends from years past, this coffee is fantastic.

- **Roasting a Cuppa Joe**

Entering the roasting area, I saw a white-clad figure hovering next to the small roaster. Pulling out a small scoop-shaped tray, the company roaster, Susan Hamilton, checked the roasting beans. "I'll take this roast a little further," she explains. "Until it gets a sheen on it and the flavor gets more developed. I'm constantly smelling and listening. I have to check the beans every second, they change so fast." Her words are punctuated by the steady clank-clank of the tray sliding new beans into her view.

Heaving twenty pounds of green Sumatra beans over her head and into the hopper, Hamilton explains the roasting process. "Roasting is an art. Sumatra is a soft bean and needs less heat than other coffee beans." Stepping close to the roaster, she puts her ear down toward the tray. "Hear that? That's the first pop."

Listening carefully, I hear a muffled pop. Through a small window I see the beans dancing around like Mexican jumping beans. "This is just the drying out process," Hamilton says, adjusting the heat.

Before long, there's a distinct crackling sound. "That's the second pop. It's almost ready." S-w-i-s-h—steaming hot beans cascade out of the roaster into a cooling tray. With coffee stained hands, Hamilton examines the beans. "Because different coffee beans need to be roasted at different temperatures, some coffees are blended before roasting and others are roasted separately, then blended by hand." After the beans have cooled all but a small sampling are loaded into plastic, reusable containers, ready for delivery.

"We keep samples from every batch and 'cup it' for quality," Hamilton explains. "That's the term for sampling coffee. It's like liquoring wine. After a cupping I may decide to change a roast. The coffees are constantly evolving."

Not only are the coffees evolving, the company itself is in a constant state of change. New coffees, teas, and spices are continually being added to their line of products. They are currently looking for organic green tea, African coffee and a new home. The small brick building where they are currently residing is scheduled for demolition. Where they move and what new products they create are stories worth following.

Review
325 words
Originally published in Seattle Magazine, *September 1995*

Sit & Spin

Is your schedule so tight you have to choose between eating lunch, doing your laundry or checking out an art gallery?

Then the Sit & Spin (2219 Fourth Avenue, Seattle; 206/441-9484) was created for you. With lox colored walls and '50s-style furniture, this multi-purpose business offers customers a cafe, art gallery, laundry facilities and before long, a performance theater.

The idea began when Michael Rose and three friends (Lisa Bonney, Stephen Claussen and Ed Sindell) looked into starting an art gallery. Realizing the economic difficulties of running a gallery, they decided to expand their business venture. First, they added coffee, then food, a theater and finally, in a burst of inspiration, a laundromat. "Laundry is quite a chore for most people," explains Ed Sindell, Assistant Manager. "We ease the burden with board games, music, poetry, film nights." (Next year, Ross hopes to add the performance theater to Sit & Spin's list of diversions.) Customers are also entertained with weekly poetry readings and live music.

You might expect a place this eclectic to fall down in the food department. Not this one. A recent review in the Seattle Times rated the fare a respectable two stars. Claussen, executive chef and general manager, brings a decade of restaurant experience to Sit & Spin, and the menu—which is half vegetarian and includes fresh-squeezed juice, beer and the obligatory espresso—is designed to please everyone.

"We get quite a mix of customers," points out Sindell. "Sit & Spin is becoming a regular community center." The cross-generational patrons include rock stars, the business lunch crowd, busy singles mixing laundry with fun, seniors from a retirement home next-door, and people who enjoy the unusual.

Loads of people come to do laundry, get caught up having a good time, and leave their clothes behind. They ought to post a warning: "Enjoy your visit—but don't forget your laundry."

ORDER FORM

Shorts: A Gateway Into New Markets @ $8.95.

Sales Tax: Add 8.2% tax ($0.73 for a single book) for shipments within Washington state.

Shipping: Add $2.00 per book for shipping and handling, $1.00 for each additional book to same address.

    Number of books ordered X $8.95 = $ _____

    Tax (if applicable) $ _____

    Shipping charges $ _____

    Total $ _____

Shipping address:

Name _____

Street address _____

City, State, Zip code _____

Mail orders to:

TURTLE ISLAND PRESS
PO Box 77598
Seattle, WA 98177

(This page may be photocopied)